# <u>How I Totally Missed The Lesson In Monopoly</u>

## By Rashad Mahdi

# ACKNOWLEDGMENTS

By no means is this a book that will surely solve everyone's financial problems overnight, but I hope that it will create conversations and motivate people that do wish for some form of change to begin taking steps to achieve their life's goals. Yes, this book is definitely going to come off a bit abstract, but I'm just going to dive in and begin to let my soul bleed. Growing up, my family and I often played the game of Monopoly. Sadly, no one never taught me or my siblings the true significance of this magnificent game. No fault of my parents, because the absolute truth is no one never taught them either….. In my Megamind voice ( How sad is that? ) Well, 44 years later, I'm trying to remove the stain of financial ignorance from my household and take on the enormous task of placing us on the right track. I've been married since 1997 to my sweetheart who I only knew for 2 weeks before marrying! Yes! My lovely wife Sakinah Amatullah Mahdi….. We have 5 wonderful children together who all praise be to God are trying to find their own way….. 4 boys and 1 beautiful young girl…..

# DEDICATION

This book is dedicated to my wife, children, mother and brothers. Also a focal point of everyone who is still going through some form of financial hardship in life and diligently seeking an opportunity to escape the slave ship of minimum wage. No! Not at all is there anything wrong with working for an employer. Everyone has his or her personal aspirations. This journey began with a small amber of deep want….. A strong want to hopefully spend more time with my family, focus more on my deen and contribute much more to those who suffer from lack of information and resources….

## 1 Navigating Through The Storm

"There comes a time in all of our lives when we say to ourselves, " Enough is enough. " We all have gone through some form of financial trial or tribulation that test the mental fortitude and resolve of us all. In my home town of Washington D.C. I have had the pleasure and stress of seeing so many troubling things throughout the city. Poverty, through observance of the homeless, the young resorting to panhandling, and massive displacement of families as a result of gentrification. Why has ignorance become the choice or the norm when it comes to being ambitious or remaining in a state of despair?

All praise be to God Almighty, I've had the opportunity to go through a lot of the experiences that I've gone through and have been motivated by the options set before me. Let us begin with the onset of financial deterioration and the very root of its location. The Public Schools and its agenda. The conditioning phase of anything is always free, but at some point, ie…. ( the point of sale ) is where the bill can become quite costly. High School is a very critical point of every child's development and preparation for the real world. Tell me why the children are not being taught about [ Finance, Power & Economics ]? Subject matters as it relates to Investing, Real Estate, and building Generational Wealth? That is the real crime being committed. No sense in crying over spilled milk. We're here now. We've accepted the hand that has been dealt to us. Well, to that I say, " the time for change is now!

## 2 Stepping Into The New Me

Once I've accepted full responsibility for where I'm at financially, then and only then will the lights of creativity and sense of direction will begin to take hold of my thinking and shape the pathway towards success. We've all heard the term before, " We have to crawl before we can walk. " This is all very true, but sadly some of us have been crawling for years. This is no laughing matter. No one stays in their 20's, 30's or 40's forever. What we have to focus on now is our nest egg for when we have reached our golden years. Your nest egg being all that we have attributed to savings, investments or any financial mechanisms that will still produce an income long after we are physically unable. I've heard people say, I'm gonna work all the way up unto the day that I die. Sure this is a beautiful thing if one is able to do so, but the question to pose to someone in their 50's, 60's or 70's is how do you plan on working? Will you be working and providing an income for yourself through your exchange in your time and physical exertion in order to get paid? Will your form of pay reflect the uptick in inflation cost of living, health deterioration and housing [ independently or through assisted living ]? All very good questions to ask.

## 3 Jobs Over The Years & Trial By Fire

I've held down several jobs over the course of time that has allowed me to maintain and sustain my ability to take care of my family. As hard as I often world work, I would always find myself wondering, " How do I always find myself in the same financial situation? " How do I go from $900 on a Friday to barely $50 on a Monday when its time for me to go back to work and jumpstart the work week all over again…… Hard work and compromise has never been an issue. I've always been rather humble and very thankful of my opportunities. So why have I always felt like financially I've been getting the short end of the stick? I'll tell you why. ( Financial Illiteracy ) Is there really such a thing? Sure there is! You've always had drive, ambition and motivation. Those were never the issue. The issue has and always will be with most folks ( KNOWLEDGE ). So what has to happen at this point in our life? Exactly what has happened mine.First off we have to stop treating ( Income Tax ) like its grown folks Christmas! A lot of us work hard all year and get a return anywhere from $1,500 to $5,000 dollars….. What do we do? The word "No" leaves our vocabulary for about 2 weeks. Two weeks because that is how long it takes us to go through our return. Sad right? It gets worst! Everything that we've been eyeballing all year just became available and all of a sudden conveniently in our price range. ( Here's A Tip )! If it wasn't in our price range yesterday before we got our money, it probably isn't in our price range today. We make excused like, " You work hard! " You deserve it! " All very true, but at what expense? Then we have that moment of realization. Due to our disease of ( Financial Illiteracy ) there's always going to be bills to catch up on! Let's not forget about that perfect storm…. Sure it's ok to catch up on bills, but more important than that is getting educated on not falling behind.

## 4 Massive Amounts of Wasted Time & Money

As I stated earlier, I've held many jobs over the years. Most of them were in the field of transportation. I've worked for maintenance supply companies, donation pickup companies, moving companies, public transportation and the famous ride share programs. All have served me well at each point in my life to help me navigate a lot of storms…. You ever say to yourself, " I wish that I would have known back then what I know now! " Of course you have! Is that the real issue though? Given all the time that we've wasted, coupled with what little knowledge that we have obtained, God has still blessed us with time. The unfortunate aspect of that is that we spend so much time sulking in all of the wasted time that we've wasted over the years that we hesitate or refuse to take action in some capacity. So let us really go back down memory lane…. What do we really remember about the game of Monopoly? Remember how fun it was? Remember the acquisition of so much wealth and property? Remember the many pitfalls that we had to try to avoid in our attempt to build our own individual empires? Sure you do! Some days, that game would go on for hours….. However, the most sad thing about that tremendously fun time is that no one never really told us before the game began or when it ended, " This could be your reality! " So now that we've lost so much time through acceptance, ignorance and trying to be overly creative through criminal activity, let us begin to rewrite the ship on where we are as oppose to where we are headed….. Sure today's job economy is very difficult, but there are jobs and plenty of employers very willing to take a fly on a lot of people who are hungry for change. Are you hungry for change? This very question is the spark or amber that will and has to illuminate the pathway towards peace of mind and financial success. In order for that to happen we must be willing to break the norms of what we consider to be comfortable, and take charge of what could be certain. Your new place of employment and your ability to be creative is the very thing that will be your compass as you begin to navigate through the storm.

[ Pennies Make Dollars ] is one serious mindset to have in order to embrace the tools that will be needed to climb the financial Mount Everest and reach its summit. One of the most damning and crippling things to ever come out of a person's mouth is what he or she won't do.

## 5 THE WONDERFUL WORLD OF REAL ESTATE

I have always been fascinated with the business and possibilities of real estate. Real Estate has the power and capabilities of providing financial freedom, peace of mind and a certain level of affluence that comes with financial success. Many people who have entered into many fields of business have adopted a small or large dose of this into their financial portfolio. So how does real estate work? He or she who controls the land, controls the property, will produce long and sustainable income residually. In other words, " Cha Ching!" Another beautiful thing about real estate is how it appreciates. Appreciates in terms of growth in value over a period of time based upon the equity and or upgrades do to the home over the course of time. This has certain risk of course as the market in real estate also tends to fluctuate. ( Always seek the help, aid and service of a financial advisor ). Unfortunately, I am not a financial advisor.  Just like in Monopoly, the winner focuses on location, location, location!

## 6 A Growing Controversy With Real Estate

As great as real estate can be, there is a growing threat that will have a direct impact on the very lives of those who saw or didn't see the dark cloud looming in the sky approaching struggling areas under the banner of Gentrification.  Those who stand to be affected by its reality are those who lack financial education, those who never really got any footing in the workforce due to the high rate of unemployment or lack of skills to become involved in growing professions.  This stability financially would have given them the opportunity to do other things along the lines of becoming financially creative.  How many of us in the game of monopoly either got sent to jail ( causing lack of growth )  financially within the game or due to us landing in so many situations where we were paying out too much money quicker than we could acquire any wealth through properties.  That phenomena still goes on today in the vast world of consumerism.  If you were to ask me, I would say that gentrification certainly has its upside as well as it has a bad side to it.  Displacement of families ( young or old ) is a terrible thing, but so is a lack of knowledge or understanding of how future generations can avoid situations of displacement with good financial education and practice. No its not going to happen overnight but there is a world of promise out there for the financially aware. It has nothing to do with white or black in my eyesight, but rather the rich or wealthy versus the poor.... So let us ask ourselves today, " How can I impact change? Educate ourselves about money! Stop looking to blame people and systems of government for a lack of resource! There are thousands of programs, government assistance with finance, as well as educational tools on the vast world of the internet that well surely enhance our knowledge with wealth and shorten the gap between the haves and have nots. It's totally up to us to commit to some form of change. Get a job! Any job! Commit to starting somewhere! Open a bank account! Save your money! Establish, build or fix your credit! Wherever you fall in under that category... Time is the most precious commodity that we have. I'm still currently employed, and real estate is something that I've always been passionate about. I've etched out a plan that I am executing to move me closer to my real estate goals, and main thing is to set a plan and begin to take action. So get back to playing Monopoly, but in a more conscious way! We've been blinded long enough! Well, I have. Whenever we desire to go into a particular field, always follow those that are learned in the field that you are interested in.... Men and women who have been doing this for years and have tons of valuable information to share and countless hours of trial and error...

# 7 Getting Back To Having Fun & Understanding Monopoly

As I still enjoy a good game of Monopoly, I'm making it my business to educate my children, friends and family members who wish to learn about this business endeavor in particular… Surely everyone has their own dream or life goals, but the world of real estate isn't going anywhere and will never be replaced physically by any machine. Well at least not in my lifetime…. Not saying it's far fetched but before such technology should ever arise, I suggest that we all get a good head start on obtaining property and securing our real estate empire. Stop thinking about money or where is it going to come from. The first step is education, because no matter how much money that you have, without the proper knowledge and skill set to apply along your journey, failure will follow as history has shown us over the years brought on by lack of information. There are many suggestions to begin your steps to financial freedom. Small of odd jobs outside of the one that you're already working. Side gigs are always good because they do not consume too much of your time and they allow your some level of control movement. In the end the mindset has to be that the hustle must balance out the struggle. Discipline has to be incorporated and maintained at " All Cost! " The future isn't as far off as we think. Three or four years will come and go by as quickly as the blinking of an eye….. So where will we be? Where do you want to be? How do you plan on getting there? What steps are we truly taking? Open that board of Monopoly up the next chance that you get and become motivated! Smile at the possibilities of what could be and what will be! I look forward to seeing you all at the top of your game and out here in the world making change! Much success to you all and God bless!

## Closing Remarks

Opportunities remember, will always present themselves to us. This is surely a fact never to be questioned. A wise person once said to me, " Rather be prepared and not have an opportunity than to have an opportunity and not be prepared…. Tomorrow may never come! Take action today! So as we return back to our everyday 9 to 5 jobs, I want you to remember to keep the fuel of change burning deep within. Everyone of us starts off with the same amount of time each day. We've all been given a sum of 24 hours to effect change. What will you do with yours?

## ABOUT THE AUTHOR

I grew up in the streets of Washington D.C. and had an awesome upbringing. I come from a fairly large family and a period in time where family reunions were quite frequent. Great times! I've seen plenty of good times as well as I've had my fair share of tough times, but I've never made any excuses. I watched my mother ( a strong black woman ) struggle with three boys on her own. Large and part I owe a lot of my approach to resolving tough problems and how to handle troubling times to her... I will always love and be forever grateful for those experiences that she provided us all with. Today I have a family of my own and I'm on my way to fulfilling my dreams. You can do the same thing as well! Keep grinding is my motto and remember to always stay focused! Real estate can be a catalyst for us to engage and do so many things that we've always wanted to do and dreamed of. More time with family and friends, vacations, other business opportunities outside of real estate, and the most import thing of them all..... " Peace of mind! " A priceless commodity for sure. Financial security is a thing that can't truly be put into measure. Sure we all have a limit, but until we find that place of comfort, we need to truly identify with a promise that could be your tomorrow..... No one will bring you your future that you or I crave so much night and day. No reward will ever be had without a sincere amount of hard work and dedication. So go out into the world and educate yourself and become a sincere **GoGetta!**

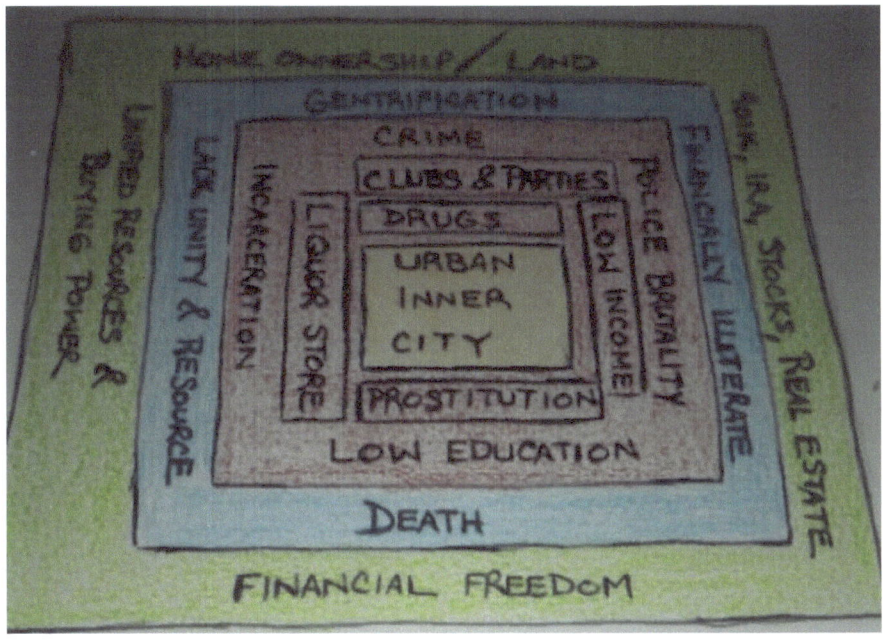

www.ingramcontent.com/pod-product-compliance
Lightning Source LLC
Chambersburg PA
CBHW041121180526
45172CB00001B/368